Edited by Shelley Turner
with
Linda Campbell Franklin
❖❖❖
Designed by Pearl Lau

THE GARDENER'S JOURNAL

AN OLD FASHIONED KEEPBOOK™

Tree Communications, Inc.
New York

Published in the United States by
Tree Communications, Inc.
250 Park Avenue South
New York, New York 10003

Printed in the United States of America

ISBN 0-934504-13-X

This book was typeset in Goudy Old Style by David E.
Seham Associates, Inc. Color separations were made by
Daiichi Seihan Co. The paper is 70 lb. Warren Olde Style,
cream, supplied by Baldwin Paper Company. The book was
printed and bound by R. R. Donnelley & Sons Company.

*Bouquets and cornucopias to all gardeners, past and present,
particularly Thomas Jefferson, whose curiosity and experimenta-
tion exemplify the spirit of happy gardening. We are grateful to
the Massachusetts Historical Society, Boston, for permission to
reprint pages from Jefferson's Garden Book.
Photographs by Stephen J. Kovacik. (pages 52–53).*

John Lewis Childs

Floral Park

This Gardener's Journal
Belongs to

hy keep a record of your garden? Can it guarantee you bigger bean yields or more beautiful blooms? Perhaps not until you've been at it a while, but it will do one thing immediately: inspire you to be more observant, so that you develop a deeper interest in your garden, so that you want to do more for it. And as this close attention becomes habitual, both your plants and the pleasure they give you will flourish.

A great deal of the romance of flowers has to do with the ephemeral character of blossoms (however much the hardier sort of perennials may endure). We naturally yearn to preserve our garden's hours of glory; The Gardener's Journal lets you do just that—so that on a biting winter's evening, when only seed catalogs are in bloom, you can turn to a photo of your roses at full blow. The effort was worth it; the miracle will happen again. And the Journal gives you acres of space to plan your future triumphs.

As it grows, your Journal will acquire real practical value, but remember that gardens and gardening have also served traditionally as metaphors for earthly paradise and for the business of life itself. So while jotting down details of bulbs and bad beetles, why not take a moment to record such thoughts as cross your mind at the spectacle of germination or the tenacity of weeds. As you celebrate the entire experience of gardening, you'll find you have made your Journal bloom, too.

Best wishes,

[signature]

and

[signature]

Table of Contents

_____
_____
_____
_____
_____
_____
_____
_____
_____
_____
_____
_____
_____

My Beginnings as a Gardener

The first flower I recall picking,
The first seeds I managed to sow,
A rake twice as tall as I was,
The first time I used a hoe.
A twilight when the grass was watered,
An August when I scared a crow,
Or the day I was first asked the question,
"How does your garden grow?"

Friends & Gardens That Inspired Me

Favorite friends in their gardens,
Favorite flowers of mine,
Here in this small collection—
From the ranunculus to the sublime!

Our Garden

Address _____
_____
_____
_____

Date residence began _____

.Total property area _____
_____
_____
_____

Soil (sandy, clayey, loamy; acid or alkaline, etc.)
_____
_____
_____

Planting zone _____
_____

Growing season (last and first frosts) _____
_____
_____

Name and telephone number of county agent
_____
_____
_____

When area was first landscaped and what is known
of the garden's history _____
_____
_____
_____
_____
_____
_____
_____
_____
_____
_____
_____
_____
_____
_____
_____
_____
_____
_____
_____

Garden Plan

Use this space to plot your garden; show location and measurements of beds, lawns, permanent planting (trees, shrubs, bulbs, perennials, etc.), position of house and outbuildings, shadows cast, access to running water, compost, problem areas (poor soil, drainage, etc.), compass to indicate alignment and any other helpful details.

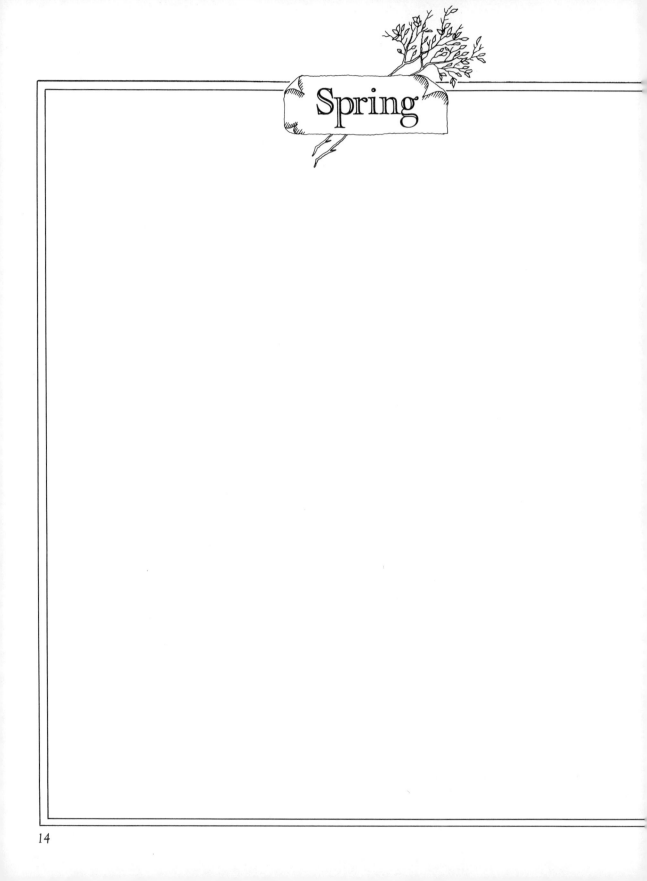

Spring

Summer

Autumn

Winter

Keeping a Record

Gardeners keep different sorts of records according to personal preference. These detail the activities of the climate, the gardener and the plants. They could also list the characteristics and needs of those plants in which you are specifically interested. From the examples that follow you may adapt your own record-keeping style with which to fill your blank *Journal* pages.

You can record . . .

The Climate's Activities

Weather
Maximum/minimum
  temperatures
Humidity
Rainfall
Winds
Light
Soil temperature

The Plant's Activities

Germination
Growth
Budding
Blossoming
Fruiting
Seeding
Pests or diseases
Dying

The Gardener's Activities

Digging
Fertilizing
Planting
Thinning
Weeding
Mulching
Transplanting
Spraying

Other pest and
  weed controls
Pruning
Picking
Lifting
Time spent
Et cetera

Some gardeners like to record details about specific plants. For example:

MARIGOLD

Botanic details
Scientific name: *Tagetes patula*
Family: daisy (Compositae)
Relatives: sunflower, lettuce, compass plant
Native land: Mexico
History: With the Spanish conquest of Mexico, traders shipped the seeds to Europe and other parts of the world; hence the development of the so-called "French" and "African" varieties.

Growing details
Type: hardy annual
Propagation: grows well from seed
Growing season: summer
Planting time: early spring through late summer
Soil: any well-drained soil
Location: full sun; dwarf types may be set throughout the beds
Water: avoid drying out, keep moist
Germination: 7 to 10 days

Spacing: plant 6 to 12" apart according to variety
Size: dwarf varieties to 7" high, tall-growers to 36; blooms 1 to 5" across
Pests: slugs may attack young seedlings
Growability: very easy
Tips: remove faded flower heads to keep plants blooming all season

You can find this information on seed packets and in catalogs, as well as in numerous books including: *Manual of Cultivated Plants,* by L.H. Bailey, Macmillan, 1924. *A Gardener's Guide to Plant Names,* by B.J. Healey, Scribners, 1972.

So, a typical entry might look like this:

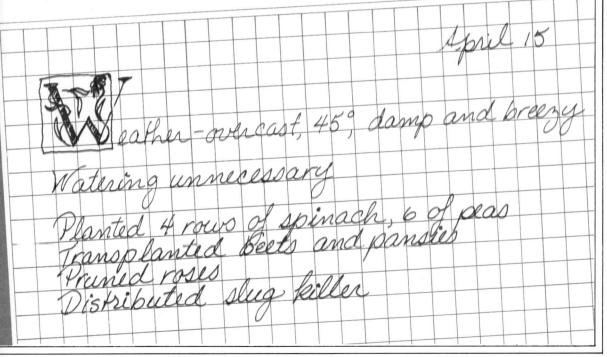

April 15

Weather — overcast, 45°, damp and breezy

Watering unnecessary

Planted 4 rows of spinach, 6 of peas
Transplanted beets and pansies
Pruned roses
Distributed slug killer

Alphabotany

f you want to try bending your green thumb to a new art, here are some special 19th-century initial letters. Use them to start the first word in a paragraph, or in the heading or title for a Journal page. Draw them in black or colors, or illuminate them with colored pencils (felt-tip pen colors show through the paper).

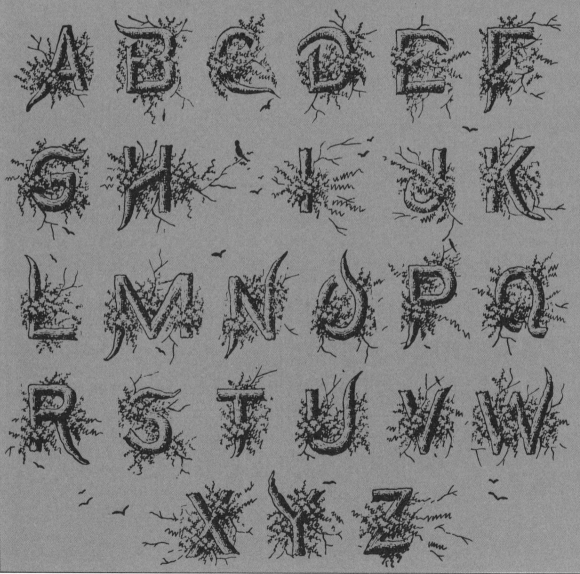

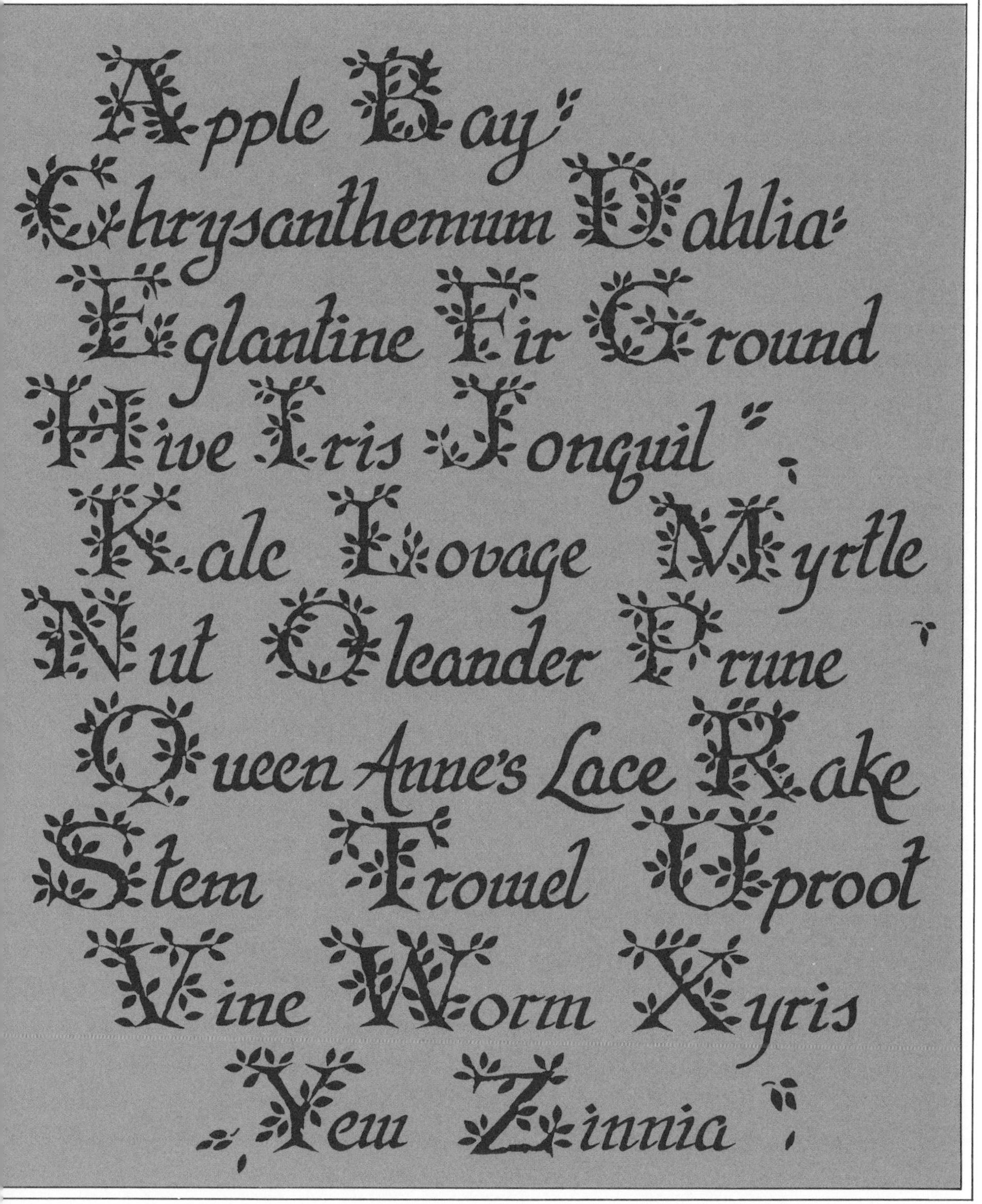

Apple Bay
Chrysanthemum Dahlia
Eglantine Fir Ground
Hive Iris Jonquil
Kale Lovage Myrtle
Nut Oleander Prune
Queen Anne's Lace Rake
Stem Trowel Uproot
Vine Worm Xyris
Yew Zinnia

Month *Dec 21/84*
PLANT ON THE
SHORTEST DAY
OF THE YEAR
GARLIC

Month_____

Month_____

Month_____

The Year Ahead

12-Month Advance Planner

Begin this planner with any month you choose. Gardening is a continuous process with no real beginning or end—a cycle with the growing season enclosed by the parentheses of last and first frosts. Because seasons vary from region to region, you will have your own definition of the 12 mini-seasons—early, mid and late Spring, etc. You can enter your master plan here, and use the subsequent journal pages to record what actually happens.

Month _____

Month _____

Month _____

Month JUNE _____

GARLIC
HARVESTED ON
THE LONGEST
DAY OF THE
YEAR ...

MID JUNE

FOR LAWN

FERTILIZER

4-6-4 OR

15-5-10

Month _____

Month _____

Month _____

Month _____

I t is a good thing for a gardener to keep a diary. At the beginning of the book he would make a plan of the garden to scale. . . . In this plan would be marked the position of the bulbs and perennial plants. The diary would take note of everything that happened in the garden. The sowing of seeds would be recorded; also when the seedlings first appear; when they are thinned out, and when they blossom: in fact, everything to do with the life of the plants. A little collection of drawings of seedlings would be of great use in helping to distinguish them another year. At the end of the book might be written the names of any plants that the owner would like to have, or any special information about the culture of a plant, or the description of some arrangement which had been admired in another garden."

From Three Hundred Games and Pastimes;
or What Shall We Do Now?, *E.V. Lucas and E. Lucas, 1900.*

TO KEEP CATS OF THE GARDEN
SPRAY WITH 1 PART DETTAL & 10 PARTS
WATER

TOMATOE WILT DIGGING HOLES
DEPER & PUT EPSON SALTS IN THE
BOTTOM

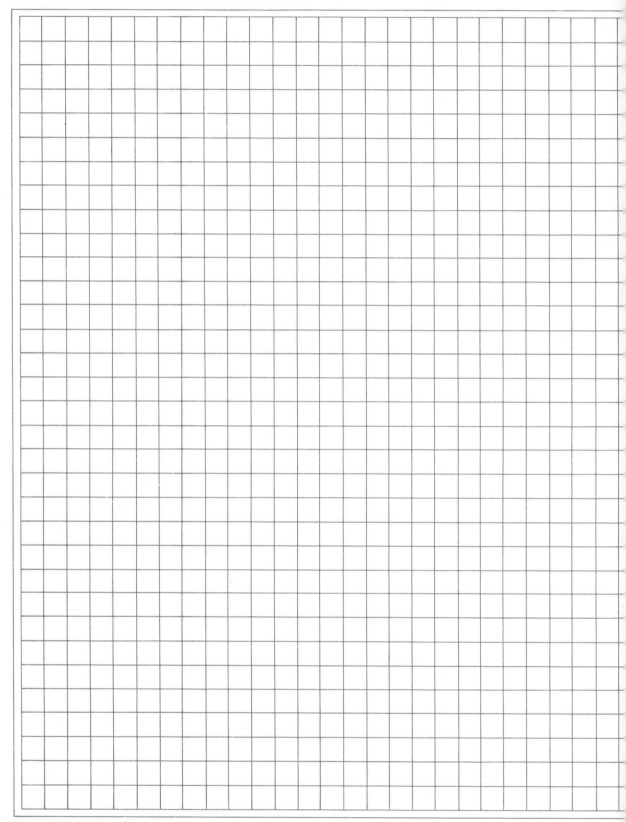

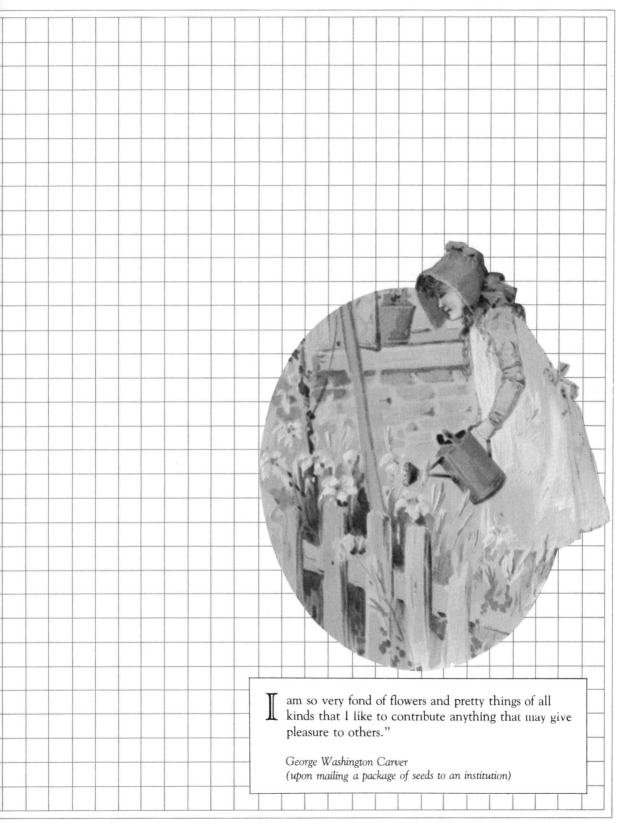

I am so very fond of flowers and pretty things of all kinds that I like to contribute anything that may give pleasure to others."

George Washington Carver
(upon mailing a package of seeds to an institution)

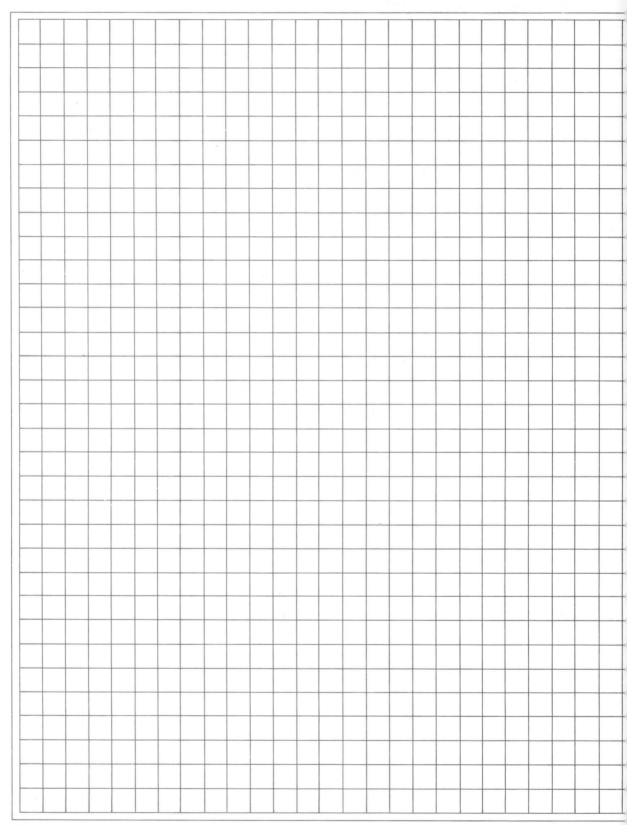

"I thank you for the seeds . . . too old to plant trees for my own gratification, I shall do it for posterity."

Thomas Jefferson, 1822

"Flower in the crannied wall, I pluck you out of the crannies."

George Washington Carver

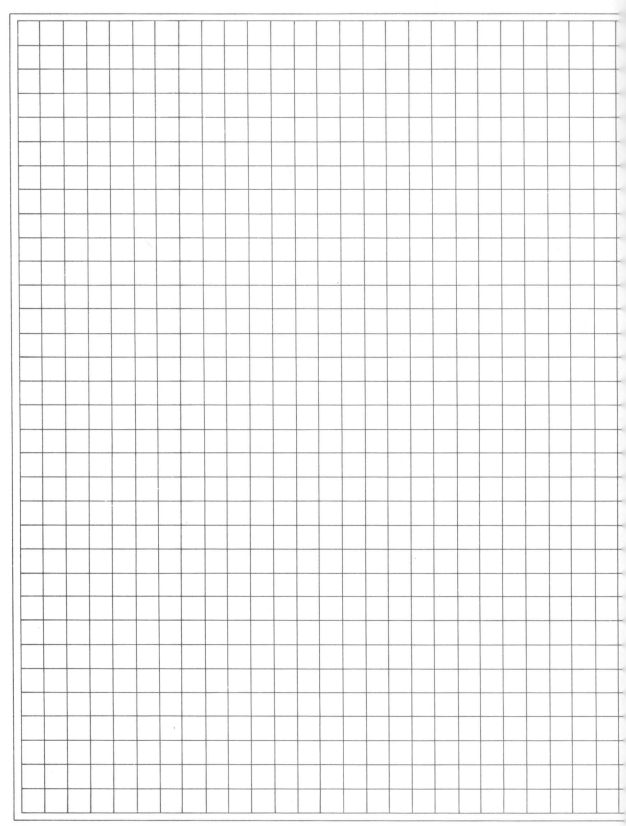

I have often thought that if Heaven had given me choice of my position and calling, it should have been on a rich spot of earth, well watered, and near a good market for the productions of the garden. No occupation is so delightful to me as the culture of the earth, and no culture comparable to that of the garden. —I am still devoted to the garden. But though an old man, I am but a young gardener."

Thomas Jefferson, 1814

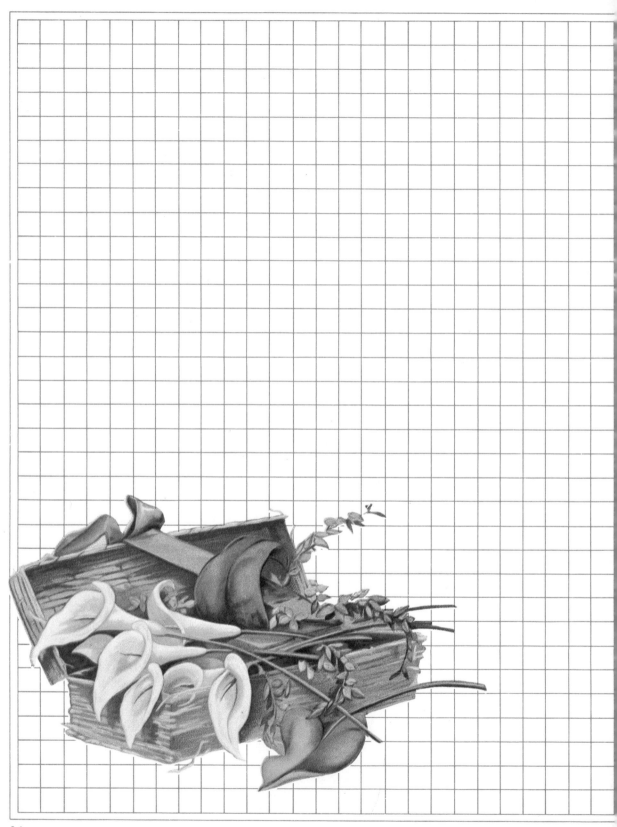

He that hath two cakes of bread, let him sell one of them and buy Narcissus, for bread is food for the body but Narcissus is food for the soul."

Mahamet

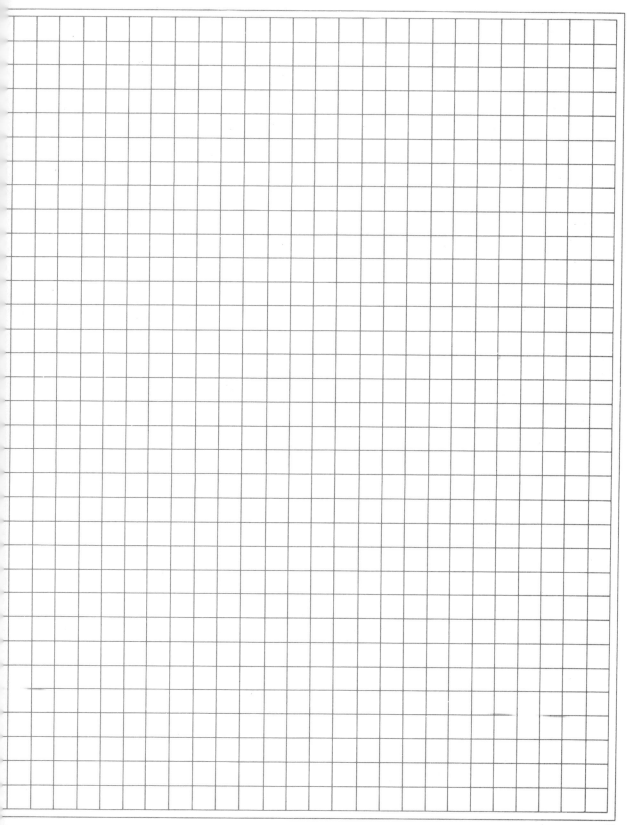

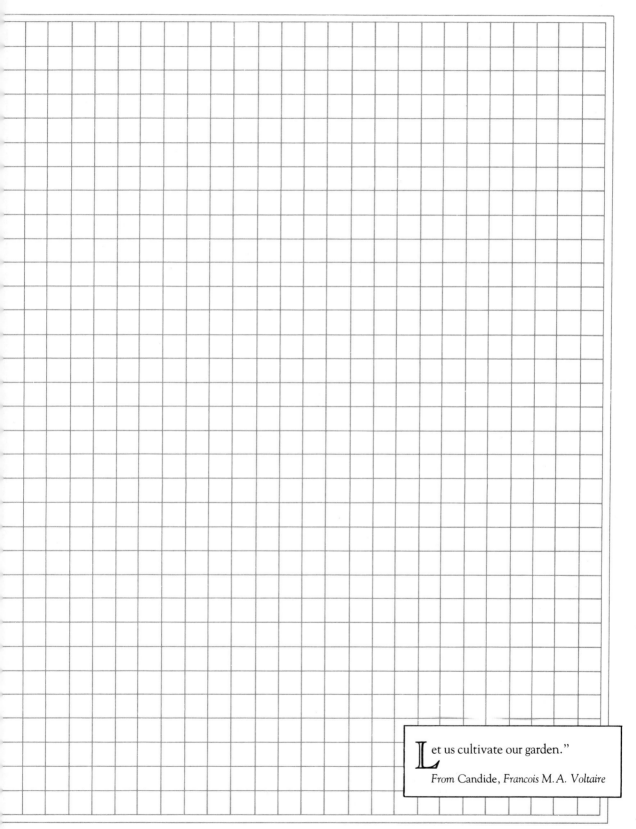

L et us cultivate our garden."

From Candide, Francois M.A. Voltaire

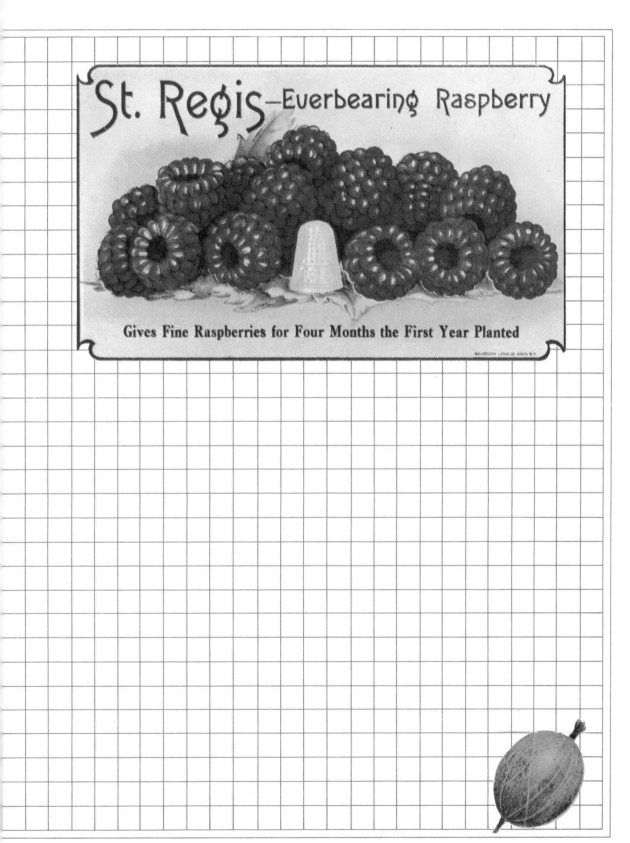

I know a little garden-close,
Set thick with lily and red rose,
Where I would wander if I might
From dewy morn to dewy night.

From "A Garden by the Sea," William Morris

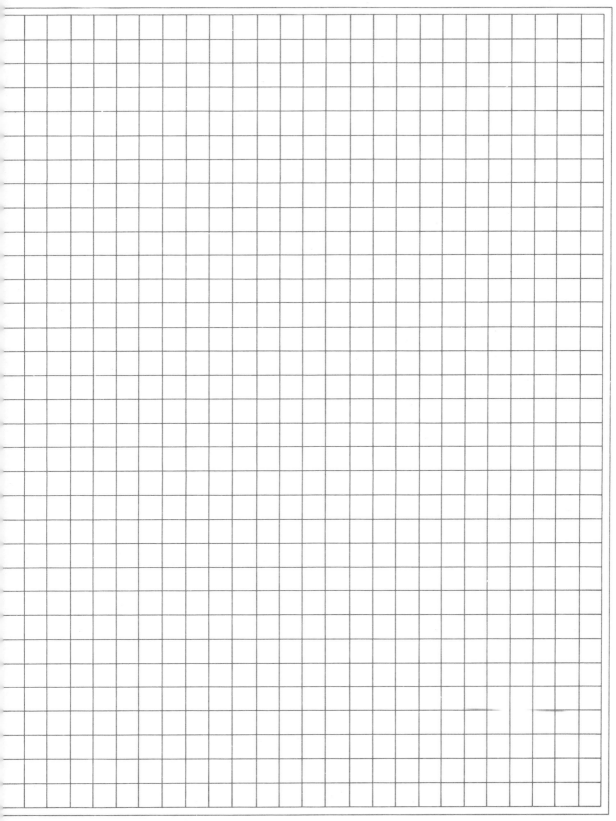

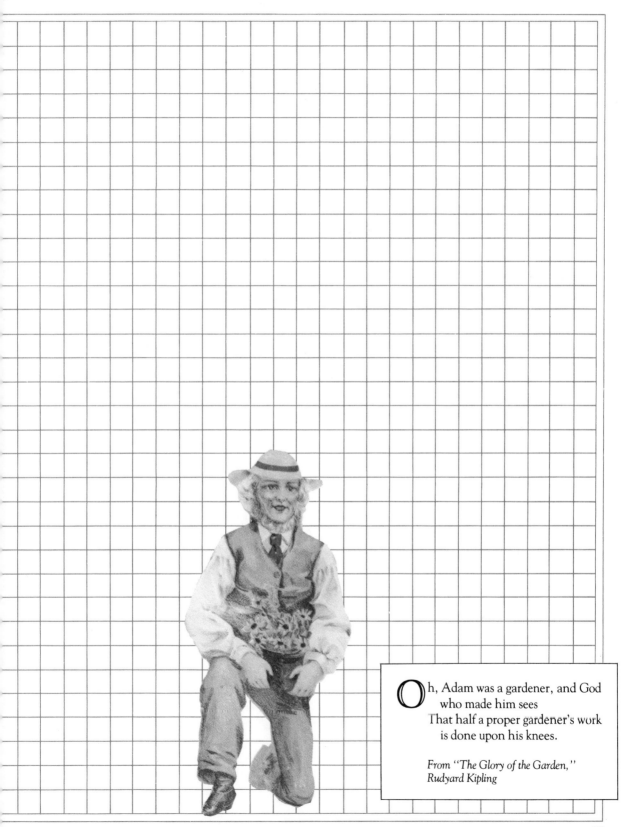

Oh, Adam was a gardener, and God who made him sees
That half a proper gardener's work is done upon his knees.

*From "The Glory of the Garden,"
Rudyard Kipling*

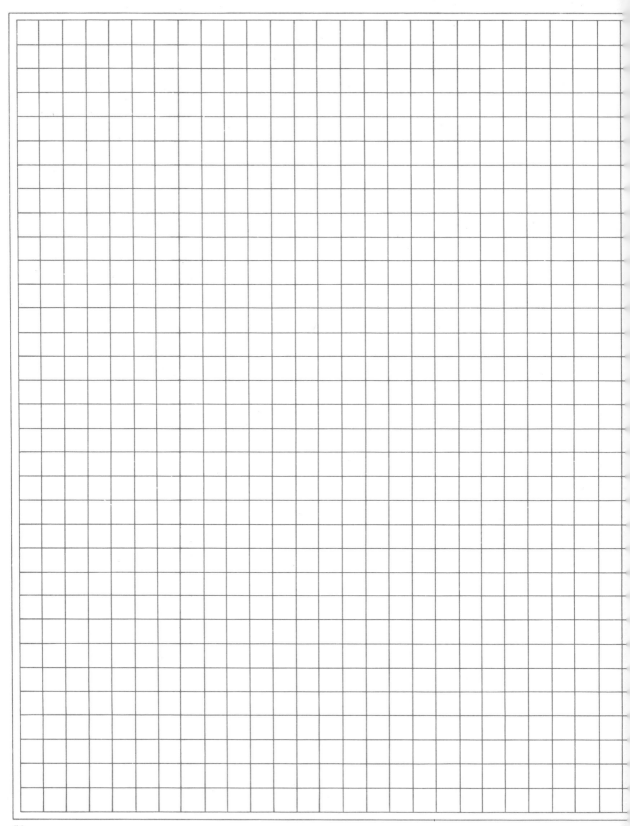

Thomas Jefferson set an unbeatable example as a gardening journalist. His *Garden Book* spanned the 58 years from 1766 to his death in 1824, interrupted only at such times as travel and high office kept him from his beloved Monticello (above left). His attention to detail was passionate and prodigious. The preface to the definitive edition of his *Garden Book* notes, "He was possessed of a love of nature so intense that his observant eye caught almost every passing change in it. And whatever he saw rarely escaped being recorded." He was equally adept at drawing garden plans—whether hastily scribbled or gracefully precise. The extraordinary record he left made possible the authentic restoration of his Monticello gardens as we see them today in Charlottesville, Virginia. The original journal pages shown (overleaf) are courtesy of the Massachusetts Historical Society.

	where	sowed	transplant	come to table	gone	seedgather	Observations
frame peas	bord. I_IV.	Mar. 23	- - - -	May 23	June 8.	-	2 quarts sow'd ago.
Hotspurs	square I.	Mar. 27	- - - -	June 5.			act gave 1 quart of peas
Cabbage early york	bord V. _	mar. 25	failed nearly				5 pints sow 440
Lettuce Marseilles	stonehouse	mar. 25	22s. May 19.				
Radishes	do.	Mar. 25		May 15.			
in do	ord. VI	mar 29	- - - - -	May 20.	June 5.		
Peas double	ord. VI	mar 29					
Ledman's dwarf pa	square III.	Apr. 10.	- - -	July 1.			less than 2. y' = 440 f.
Alpine strawb'y seed from Marzei	lower bed earthen trough	Apr. 10.	- -				
Seakale	4. aspar. bed	Apr. 10					
Tarragon	bord. VII.	12.	failed				
cucumbers	bord VII	12					
Cabbage Early York	bord. V.	12	failed nearly				9. plants transplanted July 10. to W. side sq. VI.
Windsor beans	Square II	13	killed by bug.				
cucumbers earl	Nursery	20					
Cauliflower earl	do S. W. end	20	failed.				54. plants of these transp June 30. sq. XI. of which some however were of May 2
Roman Broccoli	do. N.E. end	20	failed nearly				
Ice lettuce	do artichoke						
radishes. E. scar		20					
lettuce tennisbell			failed				
radish E. scarlet	sq. IX. 12. 13.	20					
Lettuce. Marseilles	asp. bed NE	21	failed.				of these seed bulbs, 311 fill a pint to plant a square of 40. f. in drill 12. I apart & 4 I. in the drill will take 5½ gallons, say 3. pecks.
radish E. scarlet	do	21	failed				
tree onion	SW	21					
carrots. orange	5th & 6th do	21	failed.				
beets scarlet	7th do	21	failed				
Snaps E. dwarf	V. SW. rows	21		July 3.			
Ricara.	do. NE. 5 do	21		July 1.			
Spinach. summer	IX. 1.	22					
Parsley	2.	do.					
Sorrel	3.	do.	failed.				
Okra	4. 5	do.	failed				
Egg plant	6.	do.	failed				
chinese melon	7.	do.	a plants				
Spanish onion	nursery	24. 24					
ash warted	do	24					
Parsneps	do.	24					
giant Cabbage	do	25	failed				
e. l. cucumbers	do.	26					
lima beans.	sq. VIII.	28	- - -	Aug. 19			
celery solid	low ground	May. 1.	failed				
do. red		May. 1.					
Broccoli Roman	bord. VIII	May 3.	June 30. XI				
Ice lettuce	bord. IX	do.					
radishes E. S.		do.					
Spinach. smooth	do	do.					
parsley common	NE wing I.	do.					
Lettuce tennis	2 drills	failed					
Radish. E. S.		do.					
Kale. Malta	5th			Aug. 18. 2½ row W.			
scotch	5th			3 middle			
Delaware	5th			3 E. rows			
Cabbage Early York	6.						
Peas Hotspur SW	sq. IV	5.		July 10.			
do Pruss'n blue NE		5.					
Roman Watermelon	1. terras						
Salsafia	1. N. vineyard 2. N do	9					
frame peas	4th & 5th	10.					
Potato pumpkin	E. appendix	13					
peas. Ravensworth	orchard	16.	- - -	July 26.			from the 7th. of Apr. to this day, excessive drought & cold. now a good rain.
Jerusalem artichoke							
Topinambours	E. belos's well	19		Aug. 21			

1812.
Calendar for this year.

Feb. 1. manure & make up hop-hills.
    asparagus. dress & replant.
   15. Radish & lettuce. XIII
     spinach. XI.
     Celery
     Savoys) plant beds.
     early Cabbage
     Savoys
Mar. 1. Peas Frame, submural terrace
       Hotspurs. II.
       Ledmans I.
    Potatoe.. early, strait terras 1.4.
    Strasberries. Hudson. 3d Ter. 1. a.
       Alpine. Circular Terras 4.5
  15. Nasturtium. IX. 1. 2. 3.
    Tomatas. X.
    artichokes. XI.
    Carrots XIV.
       3. Ter. c.
    Beets XIV. 2.
    Garlic. XIV. 3.
    Leeks XIV. 4.
    Onions. XV.
    chives XVI. 1.
    Shallots. XVI. 2.
    lettuce) XVII. 1.
    radish)
    Seakale. Circ. T. 3.
    Hops. 3. T. b.
    Summ. turneps 3d. T. e.

Apr. 1. Peas ledman'.. III.
    Snaps. V.
    Capsicum major. IX. 10.
        Bull nose. IX. 11.
         Cayenne. IX. 12.
    mustard Durham. XII.
    Salsafia. XIV. 3. T. d.
    lettuce. radishes. XVII. 1.
    terragon. XVII.
    long haricots. Circ. T. 7.
    lima beans. Circ. T. 8. a.
    Corn Pani. Circ. T. 8. b. V orchard.
    Ravensworths. Circ. T. 10. a. b. V orchard.
    cow peas. Circ. Ter. 11. a. b. V orchard.
  15. Peas ledmans. IV.
    Snaps. VI.
    Cucumbers. Gerkins. VIII.
    Melons. IX. 4. 5. 6.
    melongena. white IX. 7. purple 8. prickly 9.
    Okra. X.
    Squashes XII.
    lettuce. radishes XVII. 2.
    Sorrel. T. e.
May. 1. red Haricots. VII.
    lettuce. radishes. XVII. 2.
    lemony beans. Circ. T. 8. b.
    Swedish Turneps. Circ. T. 9. a. b.
  15. Spinach. lettuce
     spinach. lettuce
    dress flower borders, dig out bulbs
    cover figs and tender plants. litter asparagus beds
    plant trees. privet thorn
    dig trees into a hemp scrub nursery
      bring in manure and renew it into hills.

E. Vineyard. Mar. 26.
Terras 4. 1th E. end. sweet scented grass.
   5.   do.   a grass from Genl. Mason.
   6th W. end. rye grass. Ronaldson
   7.   yellow clover. R
   8.
   9. - - - - - Oats Scotch. R.
  10. - - - - - * do. red Tuscany
  11. - - - - - * barley naked
  12. - - - - - Tares   R
  13. - - - - - Scarcity. root R
  14. - - - - - Parsneps   R
  15. - - - - Scorzonera R
  16. - - - - Cabbage. red. R
  17. - - - - - - - - - Aberdeen R
  18. - - - - - - - - - large Catle R
  19. - - - Kale Russian. R.
the articles marked R. were sent me by mr Ronaldson
    from Edinb.
mar. 28. sowed in Square XII. beg'd on the West side in rows
    row 1st Cauliflower
       2d Broccoli white
       3d - - - - green
       4th - - - - purple
       5th Cabbage. may
       6th - - - - dwarf
       7th - - - - sugar loaf
       8th - - - Savoy green
       9th - - - - yellow
      10th Sprouts Brussels.
bed. 11. N. end Spinach prickly. (S end broad do. R.
           (12. S end broad do.

flower borders. Apr. 8. laid them off into compartmts.
of 10.f. length each. in the N. borders are 43.
        in the S. borders are 44½ j compartmts
the odd compartments are for bulbs reserved taking up
the even ones for seeds & permanent bulbs.
Apr. 8 sowed Bellflower in 28. on both sides
     African Marigold 32. do do
     white poppy 42. N. and 44. S.
Apr. 8. Asparagus came to table.
  17. arbor beans white scarlet, crimson purple. at the trees of the
    level on both sides of terrasses, and on long walk of garden.
June. 25. E. Vineyard. terras 20. Polygonum 2 staricum. sackatul
July 23. last dish of artichokes. 21. Panicum Virgatum Guinea millet.

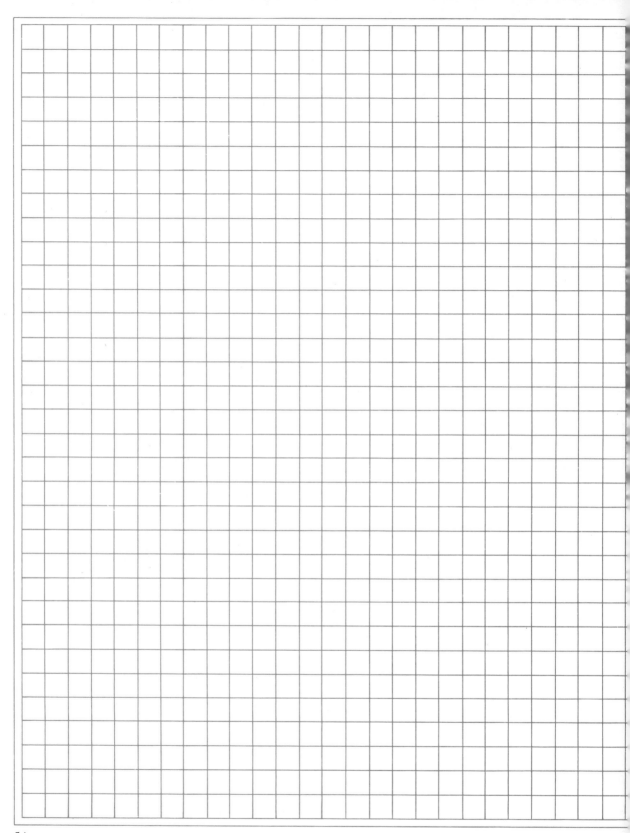

We can do anything in America we set our minds and hands to doing; if we have one weakness more dangerous than another, it is the weakness of being satisfied and complacent about things—of not getting stirred up enough over our own lacks.

There is another need we have: the need for more beauty. We have neglected this aspect of life too much; we have taken what we had and not minded very much to increase our aesthetic appetites or to feed them. We need beautiful lumbers and we need shapely and beautiful ornamental trees; we want fragrant flowers—a thousand things that make life well worth living in the shape of ornament and beauty and things that, to many of us, seem superfluous, or at least not absolutely necessary. But they are, just the same!"

Luther Burbank

W hat a man needs in gardening
is a cast-iron back, with a hinge in it."

From My Summer in a Garden,
Charles Dudley Warner

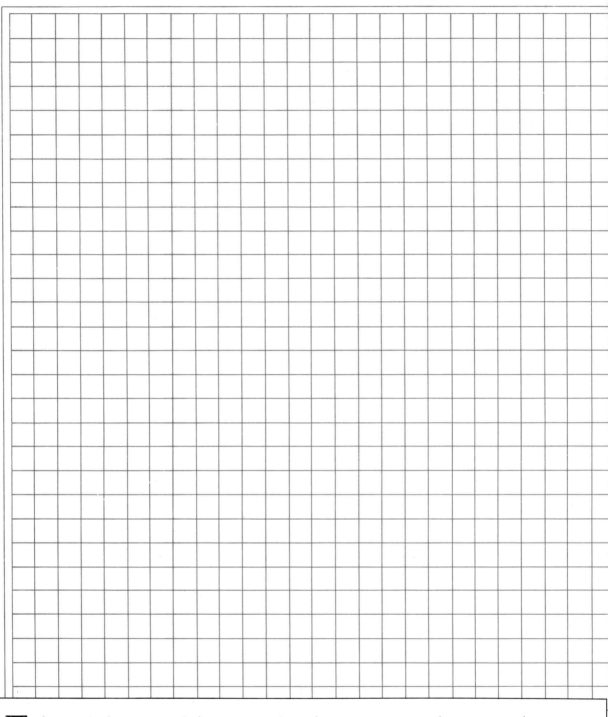

"Each spring (and sometimes in Indian summer too) a gardening instinct, sure as the sap rising in the trees, stirs within us. We look about and decide to tame another little bit of ground."

From Cream Hill, *Lewis Gannett, 1949*

Our England is a garden, and such gardens are not made
By singing:—"Oh, how beautiful!"
and sitting in the shade.

From "The Glory of the Garden," Rudyard Kipling

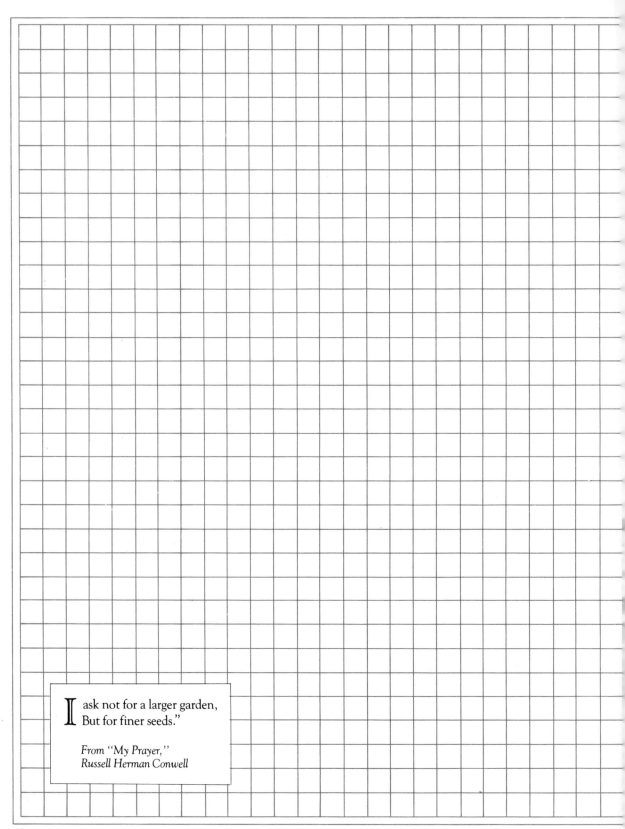

"I ask not for a larger garden,
But for finer seeds."

From "My Prayer,"
Russell Herman Conwell

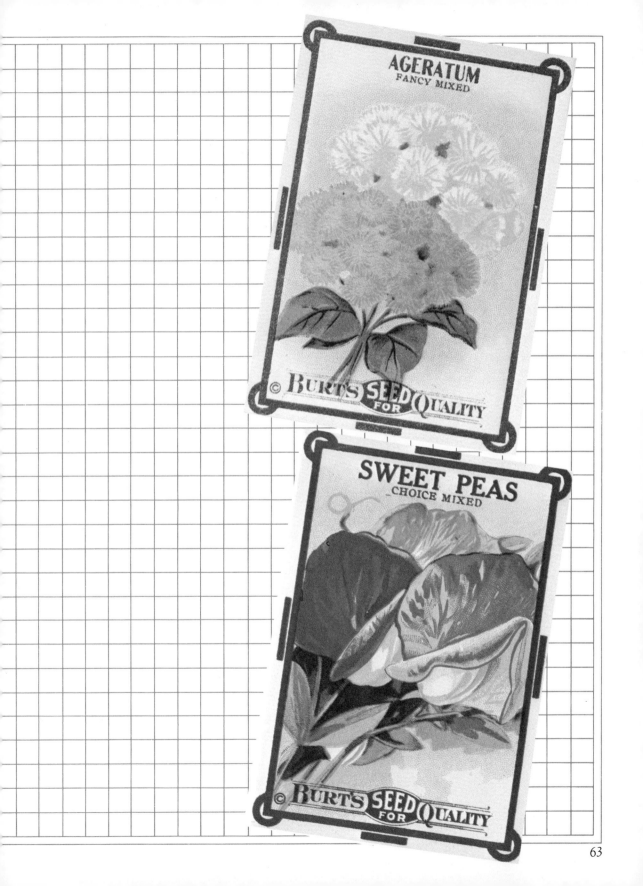

"Bless me, what a delightful prospect is here! And so it ought to be, for this garden was designed for pleasure—but for honest pleasure; the entertainment of the sight, the smell, and refreshment of the mind."

Erasmus

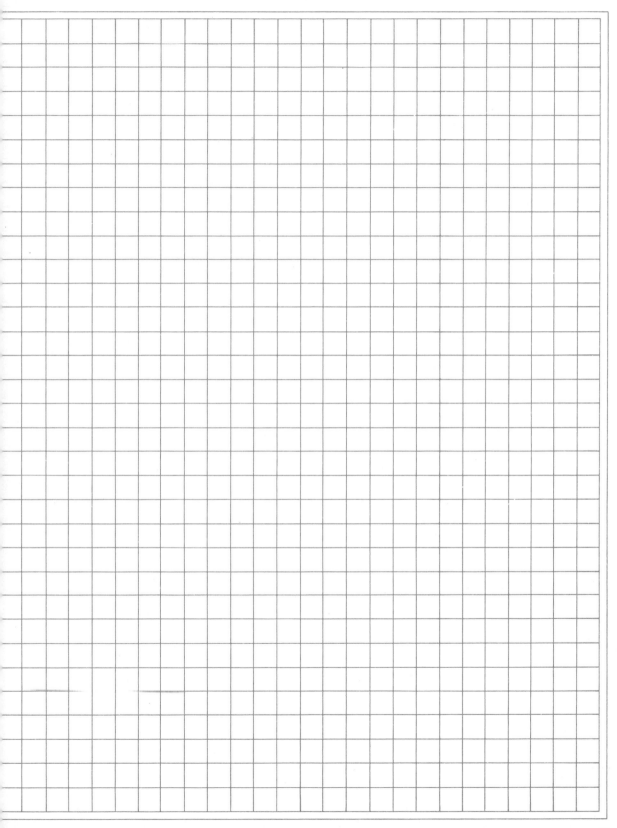

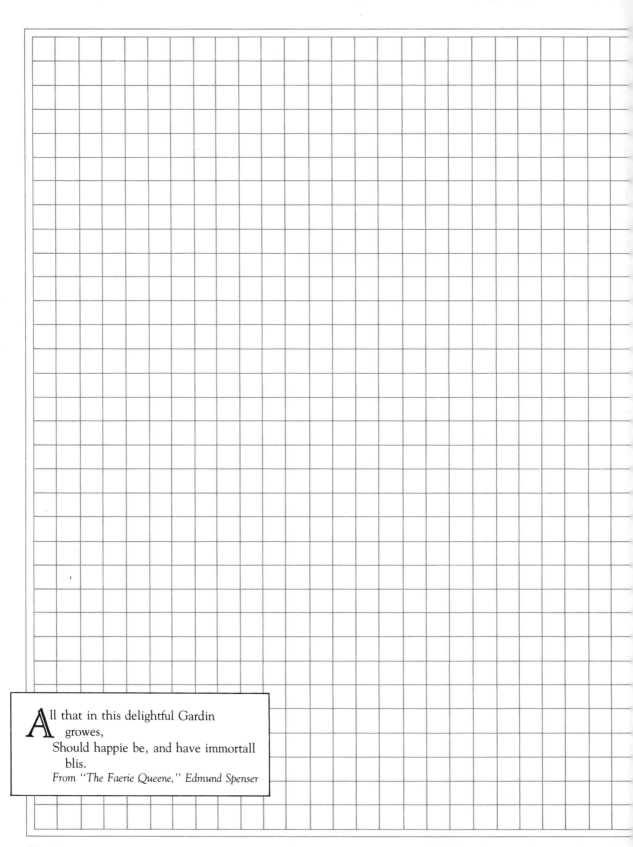

All that in this delightful Gardin
     growes,
Should happie be, and have immortall
     blis.
From "The Faerie Queene," Edmund Spenser

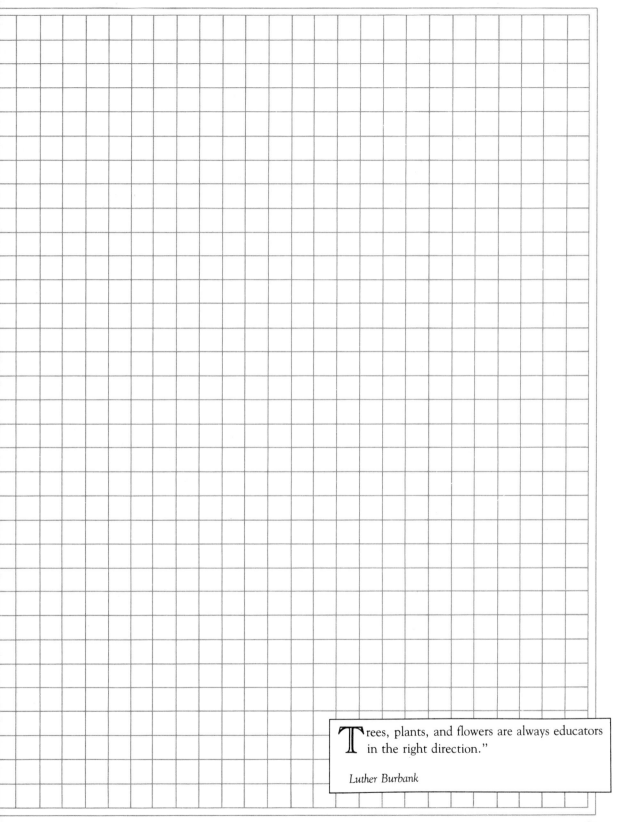

"Trees, plants, and flowers are always educators in the right direction."

Luther Burbank

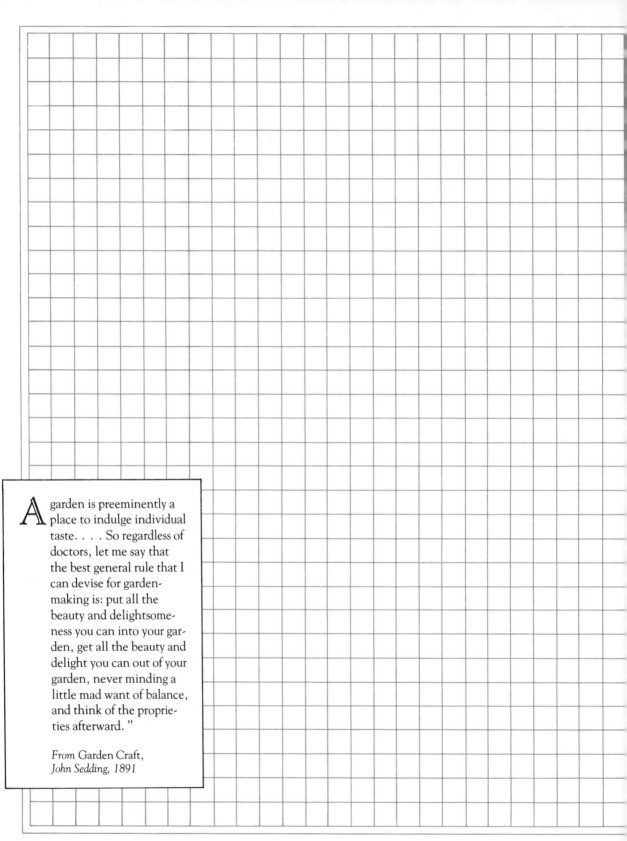

A garden is preeminently a place to indulge individual taste. . . . So regardless of doctors, let me say that the best general rule that I can devise for garden-making is: put all the beauty and delightsome-ness you can into your garden, get all the beauty and delight you can out of your garden, never minding a little mad want of balance, and think of the proprie-ties afterward. "

From Garden Craft,
John Sedding, 1891

Gathering
Cherries.

Copyright

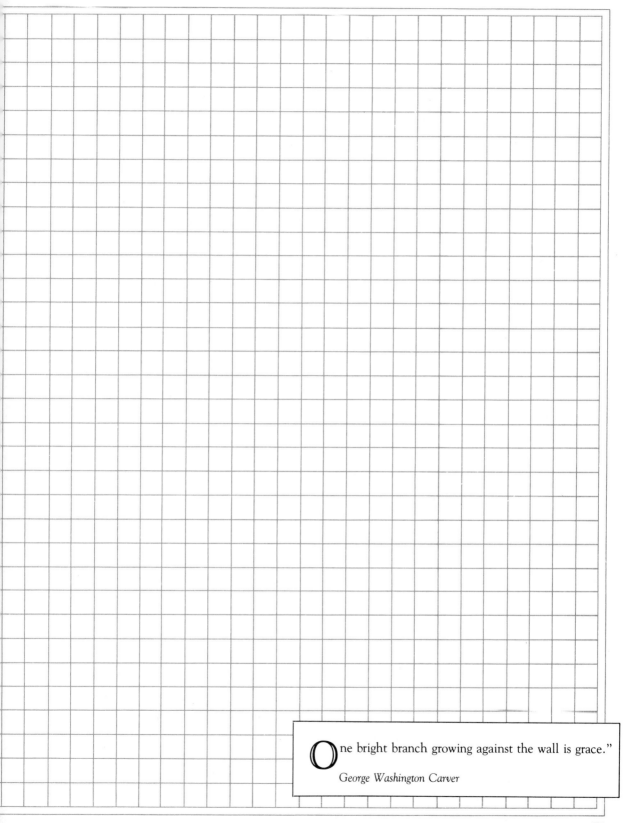

O ne bright branch growing against the wall is grace."

George Washington Carver

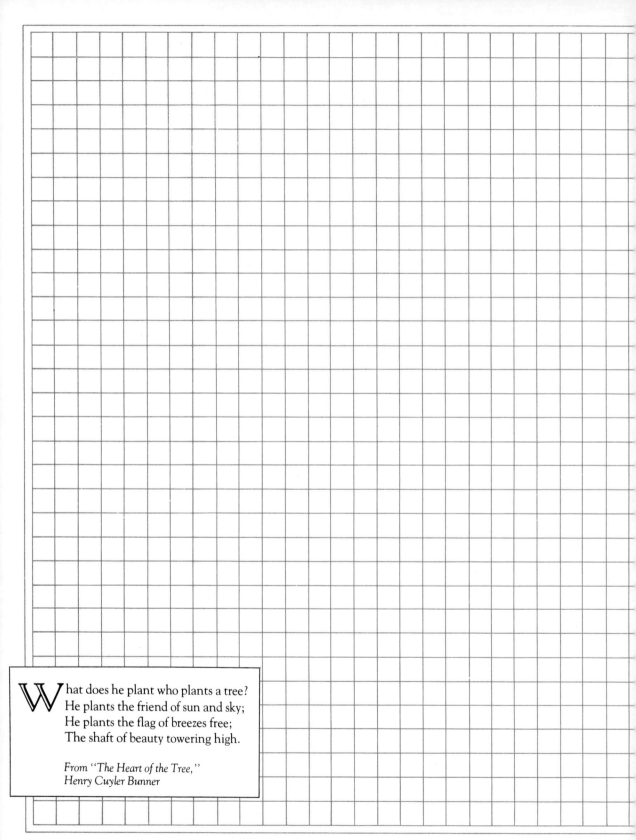

W hat does he plant who plants a tree?
He plants the friend of sun and sky;
He plants the flag of breezes free;
The shaft of beauty towering high.

From "The Heart of the Tree,"
Henry Cuyler Bunner

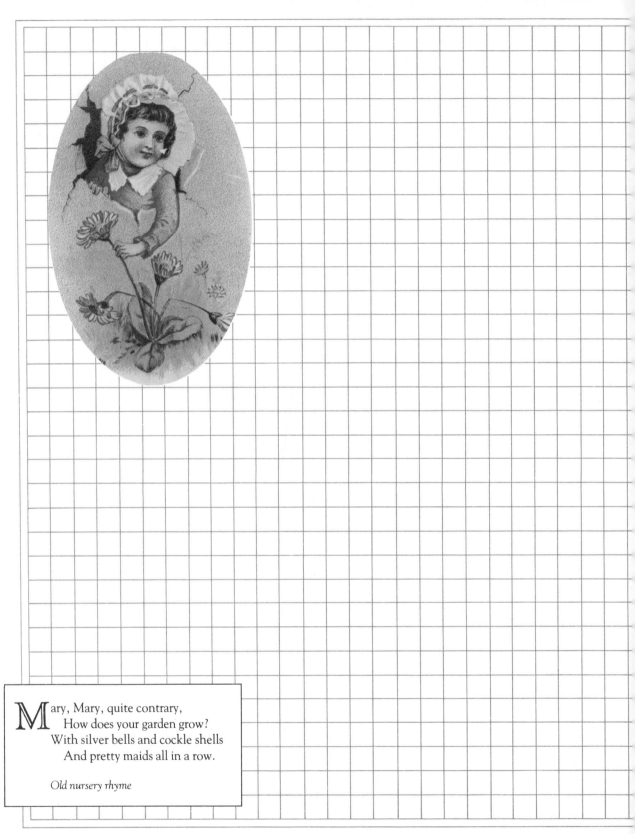

M ary, Mary, quite contrary,
   How does your garden grow?
With silver bells and cockle shells
   And pretty maids all in a row.

Old nursery rhyme

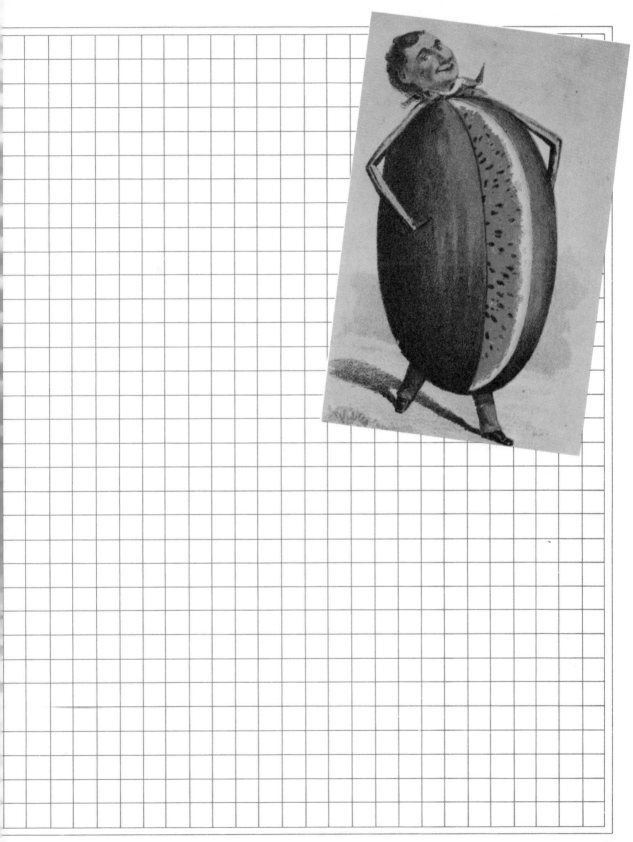

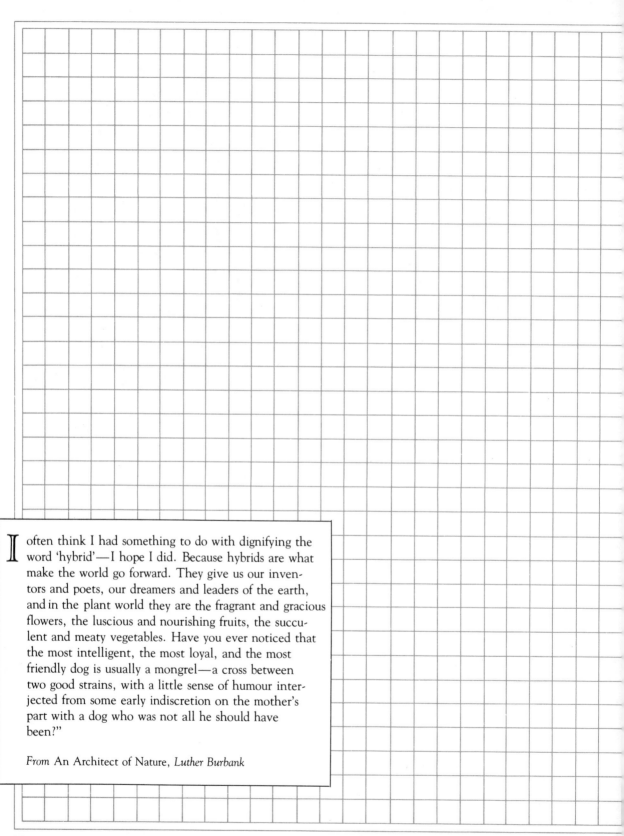

I often think I had something to do with dignifying the word 'hybrid'—I hope I did. Because hybrids are what make the world go forward. They give us our inventors and poets, our dreamers and leaders of the earth, and in the plant world they are the fragrant and gracious flowers, the luscious and nourishing fruits, the succulent and meaty vegetables. Have you ever noticed that the most intelligent, the most loyal, and the most friendly dog is usually a mongrel—a cross between two good strains, with a little sense of humour interjected from some early indiscretion on the mother's part with a dog who was not all he should have been?"

From An Architect of Nature, *Luther Burbank*

Heritage Planting Record

ustifications~both practical and personal~abound for planting with an eye to the future. During Europe's golden age of landscape gardening it was usual for ornamental parks to be laid out that would not mature until long after their designers' deaths. The patience and foresight of Englishmen like Capability Brown resulted in a majestic, living beauty that has now survived and been admired for centuries.

Americans, in due course, having wrestled civilization from the wilderness, found their own reasons to plan and plant ahead. Arbor Day—a date when trees are planted to beautify public areas—was first celebrated in 1872. It both repays a debt to Nature and invests at the same time.

Heritage planting is a bit like having your own private Arbor Day. It is a uniquely satisfying way to mark the birth of a child or other special event. A tree planted during the child's first year will be an impressive sight 21 years on~and its growth a source of interest throughout that time and beyond. If the family occasionally has a live Christmas tree, it too could be planted out as part of your heritage scheme. A neatly barbered topiary is an amusing, living monument to anything you please; enduring shrubs and bulbs are also likely candidates for commemorative planting.

Occasion/Date	What was planted/Where	Comments

Occasion / Date	What was planted / Where	Comments

Author & Title	Comments

Author & Title	Comments

Plant Inventory

for seeds, seedlings, plants, bulbs, shrubs, trees, etc.

Item	Date & Place Purchased	Cost	Guarantee/Comments

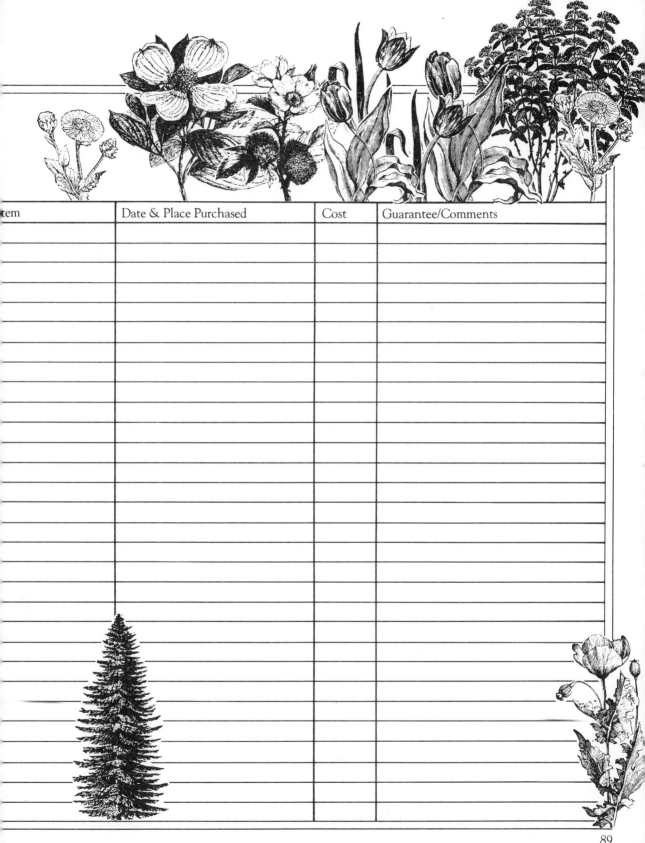

tem	Date & Place Purchased	Cost	Guarantee/Comments

Plant Inventory

Item	Date & Place Purchased	Cost	Guarantee/Comments

Item	Date & Place Purchased	Cost	Guarantee/Comments

Tools & Maintenance Inventory

List tools (including make and serial number), fertilizers, soil additives, weed killers, pesticides, etc, also special treatments such as sod planting, landscaping, etc. Include expiry dates and guarantees, where applicable, under Comments.

Item	Date & Place Purchased	Cost	Comments

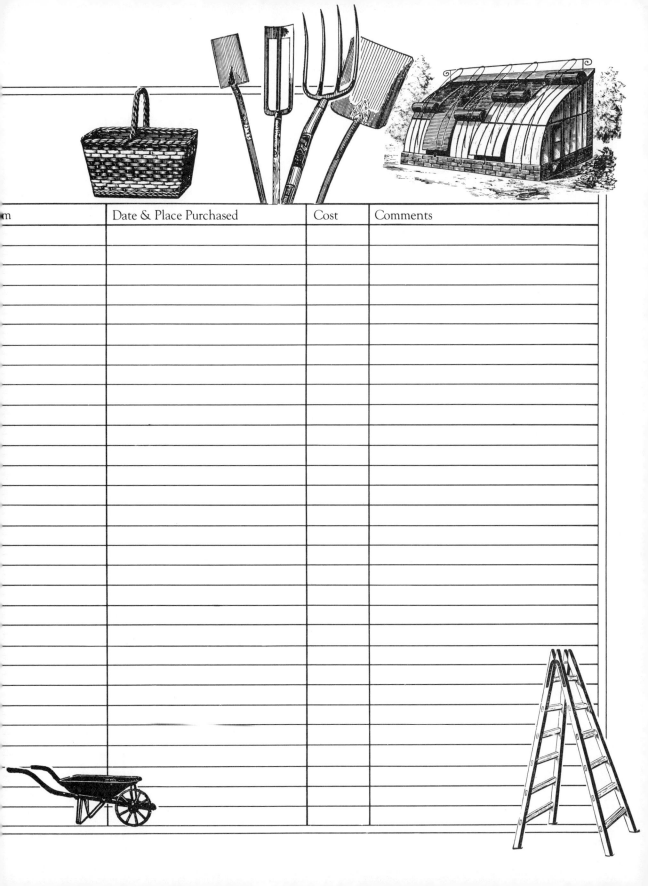

m	Date & Place Purchased	Cost	Comments

Tools & Maintenance Inventory

Item	Date & Place Purchased	Cost	Comments

em	Date & Place Purchased	Cost	Comments

Shopping List

(for plants, tools, maintenance, books, etc.)